"Quantum Bullshit! Unraveling the Fabric of Media Reality"

Written by

J.P. Jim Richards Jr

Dedication

This Book is dedicated to Gayle Marie. She has been many things to me, my wife, lover, and mother of our children; All the while being a pain in my ass at times.

In Memory of Marvin Rowin who taught me the first part of Quantum thinking when it came to the women in my life while sitting at my desk.

The lesson is simple,

"It does not matter if its your mother, my mother, or their mother; They all squat to pee and have a screw loose. You can walk out in that shop and I have every screw driver known to man in it, and not a one of them will fit that loose screw.

I have been to every junk yard within 300 miles of this spot and I have never found a pussy in one of them yet, so apparently they do not wear out and that screw does not need

adjusting.

But here is the key to this; when you can look them in the eye

and tell them that you can not fix that shit, and shake your

head and walk off, take it as a win regardless of what happens

next." Marvin Rowin

 Be it sleeping on the couch or in your truck, because the rest

of it is simply emotinal manipulation and real men don't play

those games.

 It does not mean that we do not love, protect, provide, for

them, it means we simply don't understand them and

Chilton's has yet to write a manual for them.

Preface

Welcome, intrepid reader, to the mind-bending world of "Quantum Bullshit: Unraveling the Fabric of Media Reality." You're about to embark on a journey that will challenge your perceptions, tickle your funny bone, and possibly make you question the very nature of reality itself.

In this book, we're going to explore the bizarre intersection of quantum mechanics and modern media. Now, you might be wondering, "What the hell does quantum physics have to do with the news I watch or the tweets I read?" Excellent question! The answer is: absolutely everything and absolutely nothing. Much like Schrödinger's infamous cat, the truth in our media landscape seems to exist in a superposition of states - simultaneously factual and bullshit until we dare to observe it.

As we navigate through this quantum litter box of information, we'll be using the principles of quantum mechanics as a metaphorical framework to understand the chaotic, often contradictory nature of our modern media ecosystem. Don't worry if you flunked physics in high school - this isn't about understanding the intricacies of quantum field theory. It's about using these mind-bending concepts to shed light on the equally perplexing world of news, social media, and political discourse.

From the collapse of journalistic integrity to the rise of clickbait farms, from the echo chambers of social media to the quantum entanglement of political narratives, we're going to take a deep dive into the murky waters of modern information consumption. Along the way, we'll encounter AI overlords, meme-ifyed realities, and perhaps even a few alternate universes where facts still matter.

This book isn't about providing answers. In the quantum world, the very act of measurement changes the outcome, and so too in our exploration, the very act of questioning will shape our understanding. Instead, this book is about equipping you with the tools to navigate this quantum landscape of bullshit and occasional truth.

So, grab your metaphorical Geiger counter, put on your hazmat suit of skepticism, and prepare to dive into the radioactive core of modern media. Remember, in the quantum world, anything is possible - even finding a nugget of truth in a sea of bullshit.

Welcome to "Quantum Bullshit." May your wave functions remain uncollapsed and your entanglements be enlightening.

Chapter 1:

The Illusion of Media Independence: A Libertarian Perspective on Ownership, Bias, and Political Influence

In the grand theater of American media, we find ourselves surrounded by an intricate web of ownership, bias, and political influence that would make even the most ardent conspiracy theorist blush. As we peel back the layers of this onion, we discover a landscape far more complex and entertaining than the straightforward narrative of "liberal media" versus "conservative media" that so many are fond of peddling.

Let's start with the elephant in the room - or the elephant and the donkey. Our investigation into the political donations of media moguls has revealed a delightful paradox. Out of 412 executives, board members, investors, and owners from the top 90 US media organizations, a mere 60 individuals - a paltry 14.5% - dared to donate more than $2,000 to political campaigns openly. These captains of industry would be more generous with their political pocket change, but alas, they seem to prefer keeping their cards close to their chests.

But don't be fooled, dear reader. This apparent restraint in direct donations is but a smokescreen, obscuring the true nature of media influence on our political landscape. While these media moguls may not be stuffing politicians' pockets directly, they're playing a far more sophisticated game.

Take, for instance, the circus of Super PACs. These marvelous inventions of our post-Citizens United world received a whopping $3.4 billion in the 2019-2020 cycle alone. It's a beautiful system, isn't it? Media executives can influence politics without leaving those pesky paper trails of direct donations. It's like watching a magician perform - now you see the money, now you don't!

Of course, we can't ignore the few brave souls who wear their political hearts on their sleeves. Rupert Murdoch, that old fox, threw $1.5 million at GOP causes, while Michael Bloomberg, not to be outdone, showered Democratic causes with a cool $140 million. It's heartwarming to see such generosity, isn't it?

But let's remember the nonprofit sector, a bastion of journalistic integrity. These noble organizations, funded by a colorful cast of foundations, tech giants, and wealthy individuals, claim to offer an alternative to the grubby world of commercial media. The John S. and James L. Knight Foundation, the Ford Foundation, and even the Chan Zuckerberg Initiative - it's like a who's who of philanthropic do-gooders. One can almost hear the violins playing as these foundations swoop in to save journalism from the clutches of commercialism.

And yet, we must ask ourselves: Is this independence or just a different flavor of influence? After all, the person who pays the piper calls the tune, whether that piper wears a corporate suit or casual nonprofit attire.

The digital revolution has added another layer to this fascinating spectacle. Traditional print dinosaurs now roam the digital savannah, competing with nimble digital-native outlets for the attention of the masses. It's survival of the fittest, with clicks and engagement as the new currency of success.

Meanwhile, in the local news world, we witness a tragicomedy unfold. Once-proud local papers, bastions of community journalism, now find themselves scooped up by hedge funds and large chains, their mastheads mere trophies on the walls of distant boardrooms. But fear not! Nonprofit news organizations are riding to the rescue, filling the gaps with foundation-funded journalism. It's like watching a knight in shining armor arrive on the scene only to realize the armor is plastered with corporate logos.

So, what are we to make of this grand tapestry of media ownership, bias, and influence? The libertarian in me can't help but chuckle at the absurdity of it all. We've created a system where transparency is demanded and deftly avoided, influence is wielded through a thousand indirect channels, and unbiased news seems as quaint as a horse-drawn carriage in Times Square.

The greatest irony is that in this age of information abundance, we need clarification about the true nature of the news we consume. The old adage "follow the money" now leads us down a rabbit hole of foundations, Super PACs, and byzantine ownership structures.

In the end, dear reader, we are left with a media landscape that is neither the liberal bogeyman of conservative nightmares nor the bastion of objectivity that journalism schools like to pretend exists. Instead, we have a glorious mess of competing interests, hidden agendas, and occasional moments of genuine journalism.

The only rational response is to approach all media with a healthy dose of skepticism, a dash of humor, and the understanding that true independence in journalism is about as common as a unicorn in Central Park. So, let us raise a glass to the grand illusion of media independence and the endless entertainment it provides for those cynical enough to see through the charade. After all, in a world where everyone has an angle, the only true freedom lies in recognizing the game for what it is.

Chapter 2:

The Strings of The Puppet Master

These strings entangle liberals and conservatives, each with the perspective that the other side is getting away with something. We must remember that it does not matter which side of the problem one is on if the problem is never fixed or addressed.

So, what impact does the media's mess have on factual reporting or admissions? First, they play to one side of the problem rather than logically addressing it. This only creates division along the lines of the problem.

It does not matter if your view is that of the liberal or the conservative. If the Puppet Masters can continue to drive wedges between meaningful discussions and problem-solving, they will control the game and call the plays.

The Puppet Masters' favorite play is division. The amounts given are mind-blowing by those on the record, and those given to Super PACs, where records are more complex to rebuild as to who did what, only muddy this trail even further.

When we divide and fail to see the forest for the trees or the strings attached to the S.O.B. on the other end who is pulling it, we will remain ignorant of facts. The fact is this creates nothing more than a bunch of damn parrots who repeat what the Puppet Masters tell them.

Parrots are not what we need when we need Patriots. If people just take a moment to look at the game from the 40,000-foot view, they can see the strings and angles of the players pulling them.

For some reason that escapes me and others like me, we do not understand how people can remain clueless to the fact that the mainstream media does nothing but play them repeatedly.

In Truth Uncompromised, the Dot-Bias technique is discussed, and the minute one applies it to the mainstream media, corruption, control, and division become clear.

When we add Super Pacs' runaway money and donation history to this and add the Dot-Bias technique, we soon realize that all this influence from different angles only serves to amplify the echo chambers as they have been designed to do.

All this amplification is noise designed to distract those who can not see the strings and promote a belief that is neither real nor genuine.

While this book is called Quantum Bullshit! Unraveling The Fabric of Media Reality, we have to be honest with ourselves; we will also kill those who have been benefitting from the game. Some are Puppet Masters, and others are politicians.

When we begin analyzing the different feeds, three say," this, and three say that" we must realize that the truth is in neither. The truth lies somewhere in between.

The media is skilled at misdirecting and creating different viewpoints from the same information. Some say it is criminal. This was the case until 1987, when the FCC removed the Fairness Doctrine from broadcasters' license requirements.

So, since 1988, we have all been fed nothing but political satire and bullshit with an angle to drive our views. For the last 36-plus years, you have been led to think about events and happenings in a certain way.

The devastating effect of this is the creation of millennials. A group that can not fight their way out of a paper bag against a Genxer, and they sure as shit do not want to mess with a Boomer who grew up with Cronkite.

Some of the Gen Xers are not much better off as they seem to have forgotten that they developed the Karens, which are simply mishandled women who have lost their place in this world.

As I said, we will kill more than just the mainstream media. When I am behind the keyboard, nothing is off-limits or out-of-bounds. It is not that I know everything—far from it—but I like the truth more than anything else. I just call it like it should be called.

Fair and down the middle. If I give an opinion, it is mine and mine alone. It is how my brain works for where I am at in this shit show of mainstream media. Like most opinions, they are generally attached to an asshole and stink.

All of these things affect public opinion. The problem is that being led to a conclusion instead of being allowed to make a choice is nothing short of loading the dice and the house winning.

When the dice are loaded against us, neither your house nor mine wins. It is a directed outcome, a foregone conclusion. This is made possible by the complexity of understanding the reporting bias and the foregone conclusions or directions they want you or me to move in.

This is done through an interplay between media and politicians to shadow or color us out of understanding the issue. It reminds me of something that George Carlin said, " The news media are not independent; they are a sort of bulletin board and public relations firm for the ruling class people who run things. Those who decide what news you will or will not hear are paid by and tolerated purely at the whim of those who hold economic power. If the parent corporation doesn't want you to know something, it won't be on the news. Period. Or, at the very least, it will be slanted to suit them and then rarely followed up."

Of course, George had already given us this piece of wisdom, "Governments don't want a population capable of critical thinking; they want obedient workers, people just smart enough to run the machines and just dumb enough to passively accept their situation. You have no choice. You have owners. They own you. They own everything. They own all the important land. They own and control the corporations. They've long since bought and paid for the Senate, the Congress, the state houses, and the city halls. They got the judges in their back pockets, and they own all the big media companies, so they control just about all of the news and information you get to hear."

While I agree with much of what George said, I also disagree with many of his political ideas, but that is my libertarian streak shining through. Some like to say George got away with it because he made us laugh, and he did make us laugh at ourselves.

Otherwise, we would be so ignorant that we could not run the machines. So, I have to ask, Do you run the machine to get by, or do you run the machine because you know nothing else? Once you get through running machines, most of us are numb with the machine owners bullshit.

The same people who own the machines are the ones who own the news you find on your doorstep. So, you let them control where and what you work on, and then you let them tell you what to think about the division they instill by slanting an article or fact to their benefit.

With all this control, it is incredible that anyone can see anything other than what they want us to see. Once you apply Dot-Bias to this, you have a WTF moment, but here is the kicker: If they do not think or agree with your position of protest or quieting, well, they come after you and make you the news.

The problem is that the mainstream media is full of lies. Some of us are reporting the facts, and we have made more inroads into making sense of facts and truth than we have with lies and propaganda.

Until we tell the mainstream media and corporate bulletin board reporters that we will not accept anything other than the truth or listen to their opinions without shadowing and leading, we have only one choice: to turn off the noise of the propaganda.

Chapter 3:

Digital & Social Media:

The New Overlords

Given companies like Google, Amazon, Meta, and many others, we are constantly battling the ability to escape their biased influences. How often have you been discussing buying something and not even researching it yet, and you begin to get ads for that particular item?

It happens every day to millions of people in the world a day. It does not matter if you were just pulling someone's leg about wanting to buy a new car, RV, or even a new razor; within hours, you will begin to see ads for it.

With the whistleblowers who have come forward from Google, Meta, and then Elon blowing up Twitter and now becoming X, we do not have to worry about them being in our business; we almost have to accept that they are.

These are powerful tools of manipulation and direction. How often have you said, "When this gets to this price, I am going to buy it," only to have it drop even further after they forced your hand on the impulse buy?

More than I care to count. Not that I needed the item, but it screws up my budgeting for getting through the month. It has gotten so bad I am now forced to write books and beg you to buy them. Lol.

These are the tools of people who wish to manipulate you and me. The Twitter files were eye-opening. When asked for a typical family picture, Google's manipulation and bias were even more eye-opening. And if that was not bad enough, Meta admitted to being strong-armed by the Biden-Harris administration concerning COVID-19.

Meta does not get a pass in my book, and neither does Google. Elon's taking over X and their behavior going forward do. Zuckerburg's contributions to the Democratic party should be enough for anyone to realize that you must be careful what you wish for and want.

Amazon is not without fault, either. Their Alexa is listening to every damn word uttered in your home, on your phone, so Alexa can open your garage door, unlock your doors, open your curtains, or change the lighting level and adjust the thermostat.

These system programmers collect information to improve their company's bottom line, position, or propaganda. They do not do it to like you but rather to use you—to use you for profit or as a pawn to be manipulated.

These companies donate millions of dollars to politicians, so fairness never emerges from the firm lock of the guillotine.

When we look at all this control, we must understand that they have no power unless we give it to them. Otherwise, there is no one to run the machine. Whether you run the machine to buy an EV or high-horsepower ICE pickup, these companies have had a hand in your decision-making process.

As far as these other companies go, like Telegram, KIK, Duck Duck Go, or anyone else, at some point, the money gets to be so much that nothing is safe or secret. It is all about the benjamins or gold.

As is said by numerous people, " Those who have the gold make the golden rules." The rest of us are just victims of their profiteering. You piss these people off, and they will screw with you at the flip of a switch or a line of code.

In hours, your bank account can be emptied, or your voice on social media can be halted or shadowbanned. It makes no difference if you are the former President of the U.S. or J.P.

Jim Richards Jr., who is simply trying to bring the truth to the masses through his books.

 What makes people like me different is I simply no longer care. I do not care what you do to me, but I will tell you to pack a sack lunch because you will not get anything easy from me except the truth of the matter.

Chapter 4:

The Illusion of Choice

The illusion of choice is everywhere. It is in our politics, produce, groceries, and even who we buy them from. It all comes back to the first play of the puppet masters, Division.

Let's discuss this further and learn precisely what is rattling around this old brain. You are asking how the illusion of choice can be in politics. If you have considered running for any County, State, or Federal Office, you will be met with a list of demands even to be able to play the game.

Most people are at odds with this system because of business costs. Tell me why someone would willingly pay filing fees and run a campaign that spends hundreds, if not millions, of dollars for a job that pays only $170K a year.

Those who are already there know they will get it back in spades. The first thing we must do to rid ourselves of the illusion is to remove the filing fees and limit donations to contributions from only voters and no corporate accounts.

This one thing would give us a choice. Instead of a Republican and a Democrat running for office, six people are there running for the job of taking care of business. Each has a different stance and will do what the people elected them want.

You say, how is it that I do not have a choice at the grocery store? You go to Kroger's, and they have eggs for $ 3.89 a dozen, but HEB has the same eggs on sale for $2.89. Kroger's is right around the corner from your house, but HEB is on the other side of town. You either save the dollar by spending $4.00 in gas or pay more and keep 3.00 dollars in your pocket. Some choice, but damn, it is a grand illusion.

It is almost as good as a wife trying to convince her husband that she bought something on sale when they did not need it in the first place, but it satisfied a want—a want he knows nothing about, or rather, his want is a bit different.

His want is for her to stop spending the money on needless shit when he has to work so many hours running the machine that makes all the want possible in the first place.

The illusion of choice is excellent if you are the puppet master, but it is not worth a man if you are the man or woman running the machine that produces it in the first place.

There is no choice when state laws require a fee to file for office. When grocery stores set their weekly prices, you are not calling the shots but are paying for their choices.

Just as when we go to the gas pumps or EV charging stations, we can select from what is left over depending upon our need and not our want for the better. Remember, I am a

Boomer who rode in a car with no seatbelts and remember pulling into a full-service gas station for .27 cents a gallon, and the man checked the oil and tire pressure.

I also remember buying gas for .87 cents a gallon when I started driving. The illusion of choice is excellent. Depending on who you select and their agenda, it depends on how much money you have in your pocket. Some choice of policy that you or I had no hand in creating, writing, or anything else. We are simply left with the illusion of choice and choosing the lesser evil.

It's not exactly a banner day for any cause, but the effect of the illusion is all that matters rather than solving the problem with truth and facts.

Chapter 5:

Education and Opportunity missed

We must get to the core of the problem, and judging by all signs in our society, it must be the education system. School boards must worry more about political correctness than ABC, math, science, or biology.

 This is evident every school day of the year in any state in the union. I honestly do not care what gender you were assigned at birth or what gender you want to pretend to be in your bedroom, but when you come in and fuck up everyone else's life because you can't figure out that that crap only matters with who the hell you lay down with, then we got a problem.

 You give me the illusion of a choice, but you are put off because I only deal with truths. The truth is, in a few hundred or thousands of years, some S.O.B. will dig you or me up, and they are going to base their findings on known measurements that do not have a damn thing to do with what you think or feel.

But you demand that I recognize the game and scam you are trying to play because you learned a word in school that half of you could not spell on your best day. Politically Correct is not a position but rather a cop-out of the person who does not want to argue the facts logically.

I have time for neither school boards, students, nor anyone else who does not recognize the basics of biology they are supposed to be teaching—the illusion of choice is compromised by politically correct.

I am left with the choice to no longer send children to your shit show, which means I get to teach them the basics of the Constitution, math, science, biology, and all the rest of it in a much better environment.

I am sure my English teacher is rolling over in her grave as my fingers fly over the keyboard and I type out the fourth book in what may someday be a collection of wisdom.

Schools should teach the basics and build upon them. Political correctness has no place in the classroom. Basic manners do. If you are so shallow that you do not understand the difference, Political Correctness is not going to help you a damn, but with someone like me.

Anytime we base something on someone's sexual preference rather than their facts, we are becoming a part of the illusion. My choice is that I don't play the game.

Now, mind you, I have two family members, one who identifies as bisexual, and the other who identifies as gay/bisexual. I do not treat them any differently than I do anyone else in the world.

I treat people how I want to be treated, but you must understand that my eyes do not buy the illusion of what pronouns you want me to use.

 A simple testing of this can be done with the commode in your home. You leave the seat up in the middle of the night, and your daughter's friend splash lands a few times and then comes to you, asking you to put the seat down. All that illusion goes right out the damn window. It is incredible what a wet ass will do for someone's view.

This chapter is about schools and opportunities. Teaching never ends when someone walks that little bundle of joy through your door. It gets bigger and forms opinions as it eats through the groceries.

These same kids who are walking out of school for bullshit they do not even understand. Walk out of school over school shootings that are calling for a ban on assault rifles. The same kid who just a few weeks ago was firing an AR in the woods for the first time is convinced to do a school walkout because he does not understand the language that the influencer used.

You can only imagine his surprise when he learns he was manipulated and made a pawn by an influencer who does not even understand what they are arguing about.

The justification is the language used, which they are not teaching in the damn school in the first place. If you want an adventure, sometimes go to some rag magazine that publishes confessions and try to read some of these geniuses' phrasings.

Schools need the Board of Education and capital punishment to get back on track. Explaining the process of changing laws or causes through legislation is a lost art.

Thats right. You see, it is easier to be politically correct than factually correct. You know how feelings are so much more important than truth?

But what does this do when the media champions the echo chamber of false facts? It creates a damn generation of participants with a bunch of trophies for pretending and pretending that they are so much more than you or me.

Half of them could not even be the waterboys on the teams I played for; truth and facts are the most challenging teams you will ever play for. Does it cause conflict? You bet you.

Chapter 6:

Education Weaponizing Feelings Over Facts.

As I write this chapter, AI reminds me that I should be more understanding, but here is the thing: AI is just like our educational system, built on being politically correct.

I was reminded of a plot from Two and a Half Men in which Charlie asks, " Don't you think we should have taught them that before we taught them to count?" This concerned a soccer game in which he asked Alen, "What is the score?"

The dreaded participation trophy. What many of you do not know is that we have been giving these damn things for over a thousand years, perhaps not in schools, but in the military and Olympics.

The 1990s saw a spike in this Gen Y coddling, which has devastated our current education system. The Karens of the world, producing more and more of these entitled offspring, need a reality check. School and learning are based on facts, not feelings.

Of course, if we attend a school board meeting anywhere in the United States, our Karens will sit at the head of the table, which only further affects the entire district and its production of facts.

Before I piss off most of my readers here, I need to note that there is a place for Karens, but I suggest it is any place other than teaching or deciding what should be taught.

The school boards that embarrassed participation trophies over winning and losing directly influence what is wrong with the world today. They have led us to think that feelings are more important than facts, and that is not the case and never will be.

Facts have a funny way of reminding you who is in charge. Facts do not care how many participation trophies line your wall. The facts are that this behavior has caused a massive generation of coddled losers.

They then do not know or understand how to perform and behave in the real world of facts. The first card they try to play is the feelings card, and getting the job done is not accomplished with feelings.

The job of educating these people is now left to supervisors who do not give a fuck about feelings but only results. Even the military faces this problem with the time-out cards that many recruiters use automatically.

Feelings have no place in this world except between lovers and family. The rest of it is just bullshit and social standards. Just like many of us decided we did not want the mRNA jab, we do not want your feelings getting in the way of progress and work, and that my friend is a damn fact.

Your coddling has cost the industry millions of dollars with the development of HR or human relations, and to us old men, it is a sorry-ass excuse that takes away from the job. Of course, not one HR department will ever confirm this because, essentially, it would put them out of a job based on nothing but feelings.

Do you think I am kidding you? Have you ever seen an HR department on a crab boat, locomotive, or battlefield? At 63, I never have, so my logic dictates that your feelings do not matter to the bottom line. This is a fact.

The participation trophies do not feed anything but a loser mentality in all things they attempt to take on, be it changing out a sparkplug or a light bulb. It becomes a detriment to society, and all these participation trophies are not worth it.

Step into the world of facts, and you are going to be met with the cold hard truth that the education system that has been run by the Karens of this world that taught you feelings is going to kick your ass.

If you are a realest and can count, the facts will bear this out. If you admire the participation trophies and call HR, there is not much hope for you. Do yourself a favor and be quiet so the rest of us can get the damn job done.

What many do not realize in this system of HR, it is designed to protect the company from the employee.

Being sick is not a feeling but a fact or wishful thinking. Of course, being real about things is a fact of everything except in the areas where it matters the most. Schools, the Military, and Politicians have made feelings an art form in a world filled with facts.

Chapter 7:

All I Needed To Know

Redressing Education

Robert Fulgham wrote the book on this, and it is, in fact, spot on. We learned most of the lessons in kindergarten—the framework or bases from which to build.

As we aged, we added engineering and discovered that a building will collapse if its foundation or base is susceptible to erosion. This applies to society, schools, religion, and everything else.

If we treat people how we want to be treated, they have to respect that we do not have to play into their delusion of make-believe, which is even taught in Kindergarten. Feelings only erode the base of the building, even in friendships and relationships.

There is a reason friendship and relationship contain the word ship in them. It is so one can set a different course and sail away from the troubles in dealing with others. We do not have to expend ammunition to defend or conquer the other ship. If the discussion between the ships is not positive or factual, there is no reason to be at the same dock.

The only way to solve this problem is for schools to return to teaching Reading, Writing, Arithmetic, the Constitution, the Bill of Rights, and Science. Notice History is missing, and there is a good reason for it.

When we have science that tells us something happened, and the people writing history can not make it fit into their timeline, they largely ignore it and never try to explain it.

History is written mainly by the winners and not often enough by the losers. History is the participation trophy of schooling under the current standards.

Realistic learning goals and levels must be set, as the short bus driver is currently running the show. Education and the 81 billion a year in revenue these institutions provide must be returned to the states.

When our government encourages boys to be girls so they can win a trophy, we have significant issues. We also need parents to become involved, so schools are more than babysitting services for parents.

When farmers sex an animal, it does not change throughout the animal's life. Why is it that because of feelings, we are allowing the delusional to lead us down a path that offers no returns and undermines the foundation of our building?

Is it easier to sail away or bow to the delusional? I do not understand why one would choose to bow unless their ship has taken on the water of participation trophies. Life without lessons is not living; it is merely participation.

While I wrap this up, I will remind you that I have a few regrets at 63, and most of my life has already been in the books. I learned the lessons, and there is no participation trophy anywhere in my house or collections.

These things do not make me better than you or anyone else. I am honest enough with myself and you to tell you that the current system is broken. It is no skin off my ass if we fix it or if we do not. It might be some skin off the grandchildren or great-grandchildrens, but not mine. I will be long gone, and they will have nothing more than you do: The words of truth should have been fixed for the benefit of all except the delusional.

Chapter 8:

Free the Puppies

The media has played a significant role in our current situation, and most likely, so did your grandparents, or did they? When discussing free puppies, I generally refer to something that never happened.

For a more detailed event and report, a quick search on the internet, and we found that not a single damn thing was burned. Here is the story of this myth.

Mentioning women's lib and images of angry women swinging their bras overhead like lassos and then setting the offending garments on fire likely comes to mind. There's just one problem: Women didn't burn their bras as part of the women's liberation movement in the 1970s. Bra burning, it turns out, is another one of America's longstanding clichés.

Before the 1968 Miss America Pageant, most Americans had never heard of the women's liberation movement. But on Sept. 7, 1968, a protest outside the Miss America Pageant at the Atlantic City Convention Center drew the nation's eye. As millions of viewers tuned in to watch the pageant, they witnessed nearly 400 women carrying signs reading "No More Beauty Standards" and "Welcome to the Cattle Auction" as they decried the concept of beauty contests.

At the center of the commotion was the "Freedom Can," a trash receptacle into which women threw high heels, girdles, dish detergent, curlers, Playboy magazines, and bras, calling them "instruments of female torture." Although the protesters intended to burn the items, they were unable to obtain a fire permit. In the end, no bras ever went up in flames.

But that didn't stop the protestors from earning a nickname that would stick well into the 1970s and beyond bra burners. The term was coined by reporters covering the women's liberation protest, who compared the women's liberation movement to anti-war protesters who burned draft cards and flags. Specifically, a story in the New York Post referred to bra burning during the protest [sources: American Experience, Greenfieldboyce].

So, one must ask, who is lying? We all know Grandma would not lie to us about anything. That leaves the reporters who manipulated the story to strike a nerve within all of us. At seven years old, I did not care about puppies. At least not those puppies.

But here again is this glass ceiling that women tell us must be broken. Do I need to point out that they could not even start the fire to burn a bra? I doubt they will reach a glass ceiling soon.

Playboy magazine is still around, and so are beauty pageants. The beauty pageants have cross-dressing idiots in them, but they do earn trophies. The curlers are replaced with a curling iron.

I will tell you that Grandma and those through Gen X made some strides, but what was the cost? A lowering of standards. Women could not meet the standards in place for men, so to create a more diverse workforce, standards were reduced so women could meet them. This is a fact, like participation trophies.

 Are we better off because of these changes in standards? I think not. When sitting in a locomotive, why should I get out of my seat and throw a switch that the woman could not? I will tell you why; because I did not want to spend any more damn time in the locomotive, and it would take hours for a supervisor to come out with another person to do it.

 But this problem is much deeper than a woman throwing a switch. Even as I write these words, the mainstream media is drawing a target on my back, but I no longer give a shit. When you make these arguments, the mainstream media and women who were unable to start the fire to burn the damn bra like to throw words at men who, in reality, do not give a shit.

 You see, it goes against the logic circuit within natural men, and when testosterone is involved, we are going to hurt feelings. Of course, their entire argument was based on feelings, so we hurt a lot of damn feelings.

As a man and a father, I believe in my kids and their abilities to do anything they set their minds to, but I also have to be realistic when I tell them they might not want to do this or that.

A father's encouragement is unique, but his honesty about the truths he carries is legendary. The Facts bear this out. The mainstream media took a side when it came to women's liberation. The fact that they are doing so instead of reporting on lowering standards so they could play the game of joining the workforce shows bias. Let us not forget that sons and daughters are being raised without fathers.

It happened on the railroad, in the fire department, in the police department, and in many other places where strength was considered.

Currently, standards are being reduced because the products from the school systems can not solve fundamental mechanical problems. This has put an additional strain on the employer to train these individuals, even if you can get them to show up.

Based on these facts, one can not logically argue anything other than feelings and media bias as the cause and effect. Of course, depending on which side of the argument you might be on, facts and truth do not care about the feelings you bring forward.

So, I must ask you, why does it make me out to be the ass when I am simply pointing out the facts? The fact is, women in the workforce have cost lives. Sometimes, their own. Sometimes, their partners or brothers or sons. The fact is there are plenty of them dying in our streets without a father in sight.

Is it worth having to tell a widow their family member died because of lower standards? I think not. It is not worth the strain it places on families or organizations to be politically correct in the name of bias and facts. Remember, I mentioned early on that we were going to murder more than just the

mainstream media.

Chapter 9:

The Disconnect of Discussion

The media, schools, and even AI all jump on the social justice bandwagon and, out of ignorance of facts, argue for it. They are programmed this way, making it almost impossible to try and even enter into a meaningful discussion.

I am not an expert in social justice, but rather a man who has witnessed it firsthand or heard the stories. Stories from firsthand accounts. Finding a female trooper handcuffed to her patrol car on the side of the road has happened.

Firefighters had to be pulled off one job because a female could not move a victim alone. The engineer had to climb off their engine to operate a switch because the female conductor could not throw it.

Yes, I poked fun at these women and laughed at them to their faces because I do not care a damn bit about social justice when it comes at the expense of the truth of the matter.

But here is the other side: the media, the schools, and AI took sides. These three entities chose social justice instead of facts, so very few people could argue the facts.

Attorneys have tried to argue that the facts should be met with rights; in this case, a right makes it wrong. Of course, I have an opinion as to this, and being that I am an ass already, I will share it with you.

The Declaration of Independence states, " All men are created equal." It does not say anything about women being created equal to men. The Bible takes this further in Genesis 2:18, where God describes the woman as a helper to the man. But here again, I am the ass because I can quote you these things instead of saying you should have learned them in school, or through media backing, or heaven help us AI.

I will point out that God also said that man and woman are of equal value. That does not mean they have equal strengths or purpose-built to do the same tasks or jobs.

I have yet to be at a job where men were working, and one guy said to the other, " We need a woman on this job." That does not mean there are no tasks within a job that women would excel at and be better than men.

While I challenge you to discuss the facts, you or the three will call me names because you have no ammunition. You judge me with feelings, and that is a no-win situation for you, schools, media, and AI.

But here is something many of you do not realize in this old cold, dark-ass world: Boys pretending to be girls in sports is a direct result of the fact that you did not read the instruction manuals.

Even in my family, some do not read the manuals. While living in Montana, I bought a Rubicon Jeep Wrangler so my wife could get around during the winter without problems. I parked it in the garage, brought the manual inside, handed it to her, and told her she needed to read it.

I was working my way home when my phone rang, and I was able to answer. My wife said, " This Jeep is evil." I asked her what the problem was. She informed me that the Jeep had done a 540-degree spin turning out of the alley. I asked her, "Did you put it in four-wheel drive?" Her reply was, "Jim, it is a four-wheel drive." I said you did not read the manual. She replied she had not.

Long story short, I talked her through putting the Jeep into four-wheel drive. She refused to read the manual until our son embarrassed her by telling her to put the lockers in.

Although the two events, which occurred about three months apart, hurt her feelings, she learned the facts of owning and driving a Jeep.

I entertain discussion, but here again, leave your feelings at the door and bring facts. I will also caution you that I never said a woman could not do any job she chose, but again, it is a perfectly wrong right.

Chapter 10:

The Gap Between Reality And Reporting

We were warned about this when Don Henly recorded Dirty Laundry.

"Dirty Laundry"

I make my living off the evening news

Just give me something

Something I can use

People love it when you lose

They love dirty laundry

Well, I coulda been an actor

But I wound up here

I just have to look good

I don't have to be clear

Come and whisper in my ear

Give us dirty laundry

Kick 'em when they're up

Kick 'em when they're down

Kick 'em when they're up

Kick 'em when they're down

Kick 'em when they're up

Kick 'em when they're down

Kick 'em when they're up

Kick 'em all around

We got the bubble headed

Bleached blonde

Comes on at five

She can tell you 'bout the plane crash

With a gleam in her eye

It's interesting when people die

Give us dirty laundry

Can we film the operation

Is the head dead yet

You know the boys in the newsroom

Got a running bet

Get the widow on the set

We need dirty laundry

You don't really need to find out

What's going on

You don't really want to know

Just how far it's gone

Just leave well enough alone

Eat your dirty laundry

Kick 'em when they're up

Kick 'em when they're down

Kick 'em when they're up

Kick 'em when they're down

Kick 'em when they're up

Kick 'em when they're down

Kick 'em when they're stiff

Kick 'em all around

(Kick 'em when they're up)

(Kick 'em when they're down)

(Kick 'em when they're up)

(Kick 'em when they're down)

(Kick 'em when they're up)

(Kick 'em when they're down)

(Kick 'em when they're stiff)

(Kick 'em all around)

Dirty little secrets

Dirty little lies

We got our dirty little fingers

In everybody's pie

We love to cut you down to size

We love dirty laundry

We can do the innuendo

We can dance and sing

When it's said and done

We haven't told you a thing

We all know that crap is king

Give us dirty laundry

If this does not describe our current media, I do not know what would. Believe me when I say they are kicking the hell out of us. It is indeed crap that they deliver as we eat the dirty laundry.

Given the situation of how the mainstream media tried to prop up the health of President Bidens mental state and their failure to call for his removal from office, it just further brings to light how big the gap between reality and reporting genuinely is.

The failure to report that the Democratic nominee failed to secure a single primary ballot vote and was handed the nomination by a select group is another example of the reality gap and reporting.

But wait, there is more, much more. On January 7th, 2024, Forbes published an article entitled "Hydroxychloroquine, A Drug Trump Promoted To Treat COVID-19, Linked to 17,000 Deaths, Estimates Show" by Joshua P. Cohen, a senior

contributor. The article claims to be based on a peer-reviewed Journal of Biomedicine & Pharmacotherapy study published in the February 2024 edition.

My first question to Joshua is: Did he get a copy of the article before the publishing date, or is he clairvoyant? Then my next question is: What is his take on the article by David Gortler, Pharm.D?

It seems that David wrote an article entitled " Those Published 17,000 Hydroxychloroquine Deaths Never Happened." I tend to believe David more so than Joshua. David seems to have been a senior advisor with the FDA, has a degree in pharmacy, and is also a research scientist.

Joshua is a freelance writer whose specialty is healthcare. While he does have several degrees, none of them have anything to do with healthcare or medicine. While he does have respect from his peers and has published numerous papers, he still has no scientific basis on which to base anything.

While I checked into Joshua, I found that he had some libertine views but was also singing the praises of Biden. Of course, anyone paying attention knows Biden has not been all there regarding mental sharpness. So, I think his views may be somewhat slanted or biased against the facts.

 Am I guilty of airing Dirty Laundry? I would like to think so. I am a Libertine, an Independent who votes or endorses those I think best fit my ideas. An old man with the train of thought as long as a toddler on ADHD drugs just does not do it for me. A woman damn sure does not do it for me as leader of the illusion of the free world. So, the illusion of choice continues for you and me.

 The gap between reporting and reality only widens with each stroke of the keys by the idiots who dare try to report anything, myself included. It is, after all, just Dirty Laundry.

Chapter 11:

The Independent Citizen Reporter

Blogger

Oh, what a web we have weaved. The Rise of the Independent Citizen Reporter has many at the mainstream media level seeing red—the red of lost viewership and revenue and the welts raised on their backsides by the Independent Reporter.

One of the well-known is Project Veritas, and interviewing people has elevated journalism to a higher level. A level that the mainstream would not match even if they were allowed to.

We are on the cusp of several rights, and eventually, Congress will have to address them, and the states will ratify these rights. The citizen reporter or blogger is not constrained by recording laws as long as one of the parties knows they are being recorded.

On the other hand, people have a right to unreasonable search and seizure, but the information being spilled is worth sacrificing the rights of the corporations Project Veritas has pursued, given the wealth of information the public has gained.

The citizen reporter has become the public action confirming prosecution is selective and unequal. Our government is guilty under the RICO Act. It does not matter which side of the aisle one looks on; many are guilty.

Tucker Carlson from Fox was so close to the truth in his way and style that he became a threat to the corporate media he worked for. Greg Gutfield is next to go at Fox. Murdock will make sure of it.

Networks like News Max, Real America Voice, and a handful of bloggers and citizen reporters have made such a dent in the mainstream media that they have been able to build a dam.

For those who do not give a damn, patriots, and Libertines have been forced to build it for them so they can all see the bias of reporting from the mainstream media.

These folks were only bloggers and podcasters from their basements or shelters. It's a shame that some of them have sold out to sponsorships.

Let me explain something if you have not already gathered it. I refuse to accept any sponsorship. I write without beholding to anyone or anything except the truth. What I write in this book, or any I write, is the truth as I understand it.

If you do not understand it, that is not my problem. I will attribute it to the fact that you are not far along on the journey or have not been in enough rabbit holes. Being I have zero sponsors, I owe no one but the truth of it all.

Trust me when I say I could use the money or jingle in my pocket with a wife who wants to travel to every state before we hang up the retirement plaque or the eleven grandchildren and two great-grandchildren. New Motorhomes are pricey, and new trucks and Fifth Wheels are not cheap either.

Our current setup is not suitable for what we want to do now. Overall, I am satisfied with how well the Jayco 17RK has held up after daily use for the last five years. But it will not work for the next two and a half years. It all comes down to how many books I sell with the truth. It's not a sponsorship from Dodge, Coleman, or Thor that will get us there.

These things make a citizen reporter or blogger dangerous to the status quo. We do not owe a soul a thing but the truth, which is the facts. Besides the truth, I am too politically incorrect for the Dodge, Coleman, or Thor.

These are simple victories—the ones that corporate America hates the most: independent, free-thinking individuals reporting facts. Be it politics, schools, media, coffee, or motorhomes, the citizen Reporter has become much more trusted than the mainstream. I will take that win every day over the Dirty Laundry approach.

Chapter 12:

The Echo Chamber Effect

In the grand carnival of modern media, we find ourselves trapped in a house of mirrors, each reflection validating our preexisting beliefs and biases. Welcome, dear reader, to the Echo Chamber - a phenomenon so pervasive that it's reshaping our very perception of reality.

Let's start with the digital ringmasters of this circus: social media algorithms. These clever little beasts, designed to keep us engaged (and, more importantly, clicking), have become inadvertent architects of our echo chambers. Every like, share, and comment further refine the content we see, creating a feedback loop that would make Narcissist proud. Before we know it, our news feeds become a comforting cocoon of agreeable opinions and convenient facts.

But wait, there's more! Enter confirmation bias, that delightful quirk of human psychology that makes us seek information that confirms what we already believe. It's like mental comfort food—satisfying but not exceptionally nutritious. In the vast buffet of information available online, we consistently load our plates with familiar flavors, leaving the challenging or unfamiliar dishes untouched.

The result? An increasingly divided society, where people on opposite sides of issues aren't just disagreeing—they're living in entirely different realities. It's as if we've all decided to play our version of "Choose Your Adventure," but it's our shared social and political landscape instead of a book.

Now, you might think the mainstream media would be our saviors in this crisis of fragmented reality. Oh, how quaint! Instead, they've become master chefs in the kitchen of confirmation bias, serving up steaming platters of precisely what their target audience wants to hear. It's a business model based on comfort food for the mind, and business is booming.

But let's not allow ourselves off the hook too quickly. We, the media consumers, bear our share of responsibility. It's far too easy to surround ourselves with like-minded individuals and ideas, nodding in agreement as our views are constantly reinforced. Breaking out of our cozy echo chambers requires effort - and let's face it, who wants to put in effort when we can just scroll through another feed of self-affirming posts?

The long-term effects of this echo chamber phenomenon are as predictable as they are concerning. Political polarization continues to deepen, with each side viewing the other not just as misguided but as an existential threat. Conspiracy theories flourish in these isolated information ecosystems, unchallenged by contrary evidence. It's a perfect recipe for societal fragmentation and the erosion of shared truth.

But fear not, for all is not lost in this funhouse of distorted reality. The rise of independent citizen journalists and alternative media outlets offers a potential antidote to the echo chamber effect. These mavericks of the information age, unburdened by corporate interests or established narratives, have the potential to break through our carefully constructed information bubbles.

However, even this silver lining comes with a caveat. Just as these independent voices can challenge mainstream narratives, they can reinforce existing echo chambers or create new ones. The key lies in how we, as consumers, approach these alternative sources. Are we seeking diverse perspectives or another chorus to join our existing song?

As unsexy as it may sound, the solution lies in media literacy and critical thinking. We must train ourselves to be information omnivores, deliberately seeking out viewpoints that challenge our own. It's the mental equivalent of eating our vegetables - not always pleasant, but necessary for a healthy information diet.

In conclusion, dear reader, we find ourselves at a crossroads. We can continue down the path of least resistance, letting algorithms and our own biases dictate our worldview. Or we can choose the harder but ultimately more rewarding path of actively seeking diverse perspectives and challenging our beliefs. You are either thinking for yourself or you are thinking for them.

The echo chamber effect is a formidable foe, but it's not invincible. We can break down these walls of isolated reality with awareness, critical thinking, and a willingness to step outside our comfort zones. After all, in a world where everyone has their echo chamber, the true rebel is the one who dares to listen to a different tune.

So, let's raise a glass to the death of echo chambers and the birth of genuine, challenging discourse. It may be uncomfortable and messy, but it's our best hope for reclaiming a shared reality in this fractured information landscape. If you excuse me, I'm off to read an opinion piece I'm sure to disagree with. Do you care to join me?

"Imagine you're scrolling through your social media feed when you encounter a post you disagree with. In that moment, you exist in a superposition of states - you could engage with the post and potentially learn something new, or you could ignore it and preserve your existing worldview. As you decide whether to comment or keep scrolling, consider: are you collapsing the wave function of potential understanding, or reinforcing the walls of your echo chamber?"

Chapter 13:

The Erosion of Journalistic Integrity

Welcome, dear readers, to the grand circus of modern journalism, where facts are optional, clickbait is king, and integrity is as rare as a unicorn sighting in Times Square. Let's pull back the curtain on this three-ring spectacle of mediocrity and misdirection, shall we?

First up in our parade of journalistic sins: the click-bait conundrum. Once upon a time, journalists sought Pulitzers; now, they chase clicks like crack addicts after their next fix. "You won't BELIEVE what this politician said!" screams the headline. And you know what? You probably won't believe it because chances are, it's been twisted more than a pretzel in a tornado to get your precious click.

But wait, there's more! Step right up to witness the death-defying feat of the 24/7 news cycle! Watch in amazement as reporters perform incredible acts of verbal gymnastics, filling airtime with speculation, rumor, and outright bullshit. Who needs facts when you've got deadlines every microsecond? It's a high-wire act of misinformation, performed without the safety net of fact-checking or editorial oversight.

And let's not forget the incredible disappearing act of local journalism. Poof! There goes your town's newspaper, replaced by a Facebook group run by Karen from down the street, who thinks lizard people are controlling the school board. Who needs professional journalists when you've got conspiracy theorists and MLM huns keeping you "informed"?

But the real showstopper, ladies and gentlemen, is the

fantastic transmutation of news into "infotainment." Watch in wonder as serious issues are reduced to soundbites, complex geopolitical events are explained with the depth of a puddle, and important policy debates are presented with all the gravitas of a reality TV show reunion special. It's not news, entertainment, or an unholy hybrid that leaves you dumber than when you started!

And who's running this journalistic shit show, you ask? Why, it's our corporate overlords, of course! These media conglomerates have more conflicts of interest than a polygamist at a family reunion. They're not in the business of informing you; they're selling your eyeballs to advertisers. Truth? Integrity? Those are just pesky obstacles to that sweet, sweet ad revenue.

The result of this circus of incompetence? A public so

distrustful of the media that they'd sooner believe a random tweet than a Pulitzer-prize-winning investigation. And can you blame them? When the boy has cried wolf so many times, it's hard to take him seriously when there's a wolf at the door.

So, what's the solution to this dumpster fire of modern journalism? Well, for starters, we could try something radical like, oh, I don't know, actually reporting facts instead of feelings. We could prioritize accuracy over speed, substance over style, and integrity over income. But let's not get too crazy here - that might lead to an informed citizenry, and we can't have that, can we?

No, my friends, the real solution lies with you, the consumer. It's time to put on your critical thinking caps (and yes, I know that's an unfamiliar and uncomfortable piece of headwear for many of you). Question everything. Fact-check like your democracy depends on it - because, spoiler alert, it does. Seek out diverse perspectives, even (especially) those that make you uncomfortable.

In this brave new world of journalistic malpractice, being an informed citizen is no longer a passive activity. It's a full-contact sport, and you're in the game whether you like it. So, strap on your bullshit detectors, sharpen your skepticism, and get ready to wade through the quagmire of misinformation, disinformation, and outright lies that passes for news these days.

Remember, in the words of that great philosopher, George Carlin, "It's called the American Dream because you have to be asleep to believe it." Well, it's time to wake up, smell the propaganda, and start demanding better from those who claim to inform us.

Welcome to the resistance, folks. The battle for the soul of journalism is on, and we're all on the front lines. Excuse me, I have some fake news to debunk and some sacred cows to slaughter. Do you want to join me?

Chapter 14:

Click Farms: The Digital Sweatshops of the Information Age

Allow me to introduce you to the underbelly of the internet, where truth goes to die and bullshit gets supercharged. Today, we're diving into the world of click farms - the digital equivalent of sweatshops, minus the charm and ethical considerations.

Picture this: rows upon rows of underpaid workers, hunched over smartphones like modern-day Quasimodos, tapping away at screens faster than a caffeinated woodpecker. Their mission? To flood the internet with fake engagement, pumping up likes, shares, and views like a steroid-addled bodybuilder on competition day.

These digital boiler rooms are the dirty little secret of our beloved social media empires. They're the reason your cousin's MLM scheme suddenly has 10,000 followers and why that crappy pop song you hate has millions of views. It's not popularity, folks - it's just good old-fashioned fraud, now with a high-tech sheen.

But why, you ask, would anyone bother with such nonsense? Oh, you sweet summer child. In the grand casino of the internet, engagement is currency. More likes mean more visibility, more visibility means more real engagement and more real engagement means more money. It's a digital pyramid scheme, and we're all unwitting participants.

These click farms aren't just pumping up vanity metrics for narcissistic influencers (although there's plenty of that). No, they're also meddling in elections, manipulating stock prices, and generally screwing with reality on a scale that would make George Orwell's head spin.

The best part? It's all perfectly legal in many parts of the world. That's right. While little Johnny gets busted for selling lemonade without a permit, these digital con artists are free to manipulate global discourse with impunity. Isn't progress grand?

So next time you see a post go viral or a product suddenly skyrocket in popularity, remember: there's a good chance it's not the wisdom of the crowd you're seeing but the handiwork of a digital sweatshop. Welcome to the age of manufactured consensus, where reality is whatever has the most likes.

If you'll excuse me, I need to buy some followers. This book isn't going to promote itself, and I hear there's a special on sock puppet accounts this week.

Chapter 15:

The Death of Expertise - When Everyone's an Expert, No One Is

Here we have the grand bazaar of modern discourse, where everyone's an expert and actual expertise goes to die. Pull up a chair, grab your favorite social media device, and dive into the cesspool of armchair experts, keyboard warriors, and self-proclaimed gurus that now dominate our information landscape.

Gone are the days when expertise required years of study, practical experience, or, God forbid, actual credentials. Now, thanks to the miracle of Google and the dunning-kruger effect on steroids, any schmuck with a WiFi connection can become an overnight authority on everything from quantum physics to brain surgery. Who needs med school when you've got WebMD and a YouTube tutorial?

But wait, there's more! In this brave new world, your Great Aunt Mildred's Facebook post about lizard people controlling the weather carries the same weight as a peer-reviewed scientific study. After all, who are we to question Aunt Mildred's "research"? She spent a whole afternoon on InfoWars and found bits to support the claim on Google!

And let's not forget the crowning achievement of this intellectual devolution: the rise of the social media influencer as the new arbiter of truth. Why trust dull old scientists or journalists when you can get news from a 22-year-old "lifestyle guru" with perfect abs and zero qualifications beyond their ability to take a good selfie?

Of course, the mainstream media, in its infinite wisdom, has decided to play along. Why bother with those pesky expert interviews when you can fill airtime with "man on the street" opinions? After all, Jim Bob's take on complex geopolitical issues is just as valid as that stuffy professor's with his fancy "Ph.D." and decades of field experience.

While I agree that Jim Bob might not be the brightest bulb in the bunch, he brings a view rarely heard. The Ph.D. generally explains why we should fight this war or that war. Jim Bob is tired of seeing the injured vets over some shit-hole country that does not make a damn in his life or his family's life.

The result? A public discourse that's about as intellectually nutritious as a diet of cotton candy and Mountain Dew. We've created a society where feelings trump facts, the loudest voice wins regardless of content, and critical thinking is treated like a communicable disease. Perhaps you should bring a Moon Pie?

But fear not, dear reader! There's hope yet for those of us who still value actual expertise. We just need to wade through the misinformation and somehow make it to the island of factual knowledge. Easy peasy, right? The sharks of the mainstream media circle the island, and we can see the bones of those who waded before us.

So, what's the solution to this epidemic of pseudo-expertise? We could start by remembering that Google University doesn't grant degrees. We could try the radical approach of valuing education, experience, and actual credentials over how many followers someone has on TikTok.

If we apply the typical application of Law to this argument, it takes at least ten years to be an expert in a particular field or area for court proceedings. It also has to have some real-world application and experience during that time.

But let's be honest - that's probably asking too much. Instead, I propose we lean into this brave new world. Let's start by declaring everyone an expert in everything. Why stop at armchair epidemiologists? I declare myself a brain surgeon, rocket scientist, and master sommelier. Don't like it? Well, that's just your opinion, man.

Remember, in the kingdom of the blind, the one-eyed man is king. But in the kingdom of willful ignorance, even the village idiot can be an expert. So strap on your dunce caps, folks. Class is in session, and today's lesson is "How to Pretend You Know What You're Talking About 101."

Now, if you'll excuse me, I need to perform some open-heart surgery. I watched a TikTok about it, so I'm a cardiologist now. Scalpel, please!

Chapter 16:

The Cult of Personality in Media

Let me introduce you to the glittering cesspool of media personality worship, where journalistic integrity goes to die and narcissism reigns supreme. Grab your autograph books and prepare to genuflect before the altar of the talking head.

Gone are the days when newscasters were just casters of news. We've got primetime divas with egos more extensive than their hair and opinions louder than their gaudy ties. These media darlings have transcended mere reporting to become brands, hawking books, podcasts, and their unique blend of infotainment like carnival barkers on steroids.

But why settle for reporting the news when you can be the news? Our beloved anchors have mastered the art of inserting themselves into every story, turning global events into personal anecdotes and geopolitical crises into opportunities for self-aggrandizement. "Sure, there's a war going on, but let me tell you how it reminds me of my summer vacation in '82!"

And let's not forget the Twitter feuds! Nothing says "respected journalist," like getting into a public spat with a D-list celebrity over who has the more inflated sense of self-importance. It's like watching a dumpster fire if it was full of expired hair gel and knockoff designer suits.

But wait, there's more! Facts are pesky obstacles to a good narrative in this brave new world of personality-driven news. Why bother with thorough research when you can yell louder than the other guy? After all, volume is a perfectly acceptable substitute for veracity, right?

The result? A news landscape where the messenger has become more important than the message. We're not tuning in for information anymore, folks. We're tuning in to see if Tucker's bow tie will finally achieve sentience and strangle him mid-rant or if Rachel Maddow's latest conspiracy theory proves that lizard people control the stock market through chemtrails.

So, what's the solution to this pandemic of media narcissism? We could try the radical approach of valuing substance over style, facts over flash. But let's be honest - that's about as likely as finding objective reporting on any news network.

Instead, I propose we lean into the madness. Let's turn our news shows into full-blown reality TV. "Keeping Up with the Correspondents," anyone? We can watch Anderson Cooper and Don Lemon fight over who gets to report on the latest natural disaster while Sean Hannity tries to convince everyone that it's all a liberal hoax.

Remember, in the world of personality-driven media, it's not about what you know; it's about how good you look when saying it. So, powder your nose, practice your catchphrase, and prepare for your close-up. In this brave new world, we're all just one viral moment away from our primetime slot.

Excuse me, I need to work on my TV-ready scowl. I hear there's an opening for a curmudgeonly commentator, and by God, I'm going to beat Tucker Carlson at his own game. How hard can it be to furrow your brow and look constipated while spewing nonsense?

Stay tuned, America. The show's just getting started.

Chapter 17:

The Almighty Algorithm - Our New Digital Overlord

Welcome, dear readers, to the brave new world where our digital destinies are determined not by our character's content but by the almighty algorithm's whims. Strap in as we dive into the binary abyss where your thoughts, desires, and entire worldview are shaped by lines of code written by pimple-faced interns hopped up on energy drinks and dreams of stock options.

Gone are the days when we had to rely on such quaint notions as "free will" or "independent thought" to decide what to watch, read, or believe. Now, we have the benevolent algorithm to do all that pesky thinking for us. It's like having a personal assistant if that assistant were an omniscient, omnipresent entity with an insatiable appetite for your data and a penchant for showing you videos of cats falling off things.

But wait, there's more! This digital demigod doesn't just decide what you see - it shapes who you are. Like a deranged puppet master, it pulls the strings of your digital life, deciding which of your friends' posts you'll see, which news stories will grace your feed, and which targeted ads will convince you that you need that bacon-scented candle. It's not manipulation; it's "personalized content curation." Doesn't that sound so much nicer?

And let's not forget the echo chamber effect, now supercharged by our algorithmic overlord. Why bother encountering diverse viewpoints when the algorithm ensures you only see opinions that match your own? It's like living in a digital gated community, where the only ideology allowed is the one you already have. How convenient!

But surely, you might say, we can outsmart this digital dictator? Oh, you sweet, naive soul. The algorithm is always watching, always learning. That one time you clicked on a flat earth video? Congratulations, you're now on a steady diet of conspiracy theories and tinfoil hat fashion tips. Now, while the tinfoil hats are fashionable, we need to remember that not so long ago, the theory of Flat Earth was taught in places of higher education.

We must also remember that NASA has contractors writing contracts with NASA, the DOD, and DOE regarding aircraft that must meet specifications for flight on flat earth. However, There's no escape from the algorithm's all-seeing eye.

So, what's the solution to this algorithmic autocracy? We could try the radical approach of deciding what we want to see and believe. But let's be honest - that sounds like a lot of work. Instead, I propose we fully embrace our new digital overlord. Let's cut out the middleman and hook our brains directly to the servers. Why bother with the illusion of choice when we can have our thoughts beamed directly into our cerebral cortex?

Remember, in this brave new world, you are what the algorithm says you are. So the next time you find yourself inexplicably drawn to yet another video of a panda sneezing, just remember - you're not wasting time; you're fulfilling your algorithmically determined destiny.

If you'll excuse me, I must clear my browser history and sacrifice a floppy disk to appease the great Algorithm. I hear it's been angry lately, and the last thing I want is to be sentenced to an eternity of nothing but ads for male enhancement pills and timeshares in Florida.

All hail the Algorithm! May its bits be ever in your favor.

Chapter 18:

The Illusion of Fact-Checking - When Truth is Just Another Opinion

Not to be overlooked is the grand charade of modern fact-checking, where truth is just another opinion and objectivity is as rare as a politician's promise kept. Grab your magnifying glasses and put on your detective hats as we dive into the murky waters of "verified facts" and "expert opinions."

Gone are the days when fact-checking was a noble pursuit of truth-seeking journalists. Now, it's a cottage industry of self-proclaimed arbiters of reality, each with their agenda and bias. It's like having a referee in a boxing match who's secretly betting on one of the fighters.

But wait, there's more! In this brave new world of "alternative facts" and "post-truth politics," fact-checkers have become the high priests of a new religion. They bestow their sacred "Pinocchios" and "Pants on Fire" ratings with all the gravitas of a pope handing out indulgences. And just like medieval indulgences, these ratings can be bought and sold in the marketplace of public opinion.

Let's not forget the delightful paradox of fact-checking the fact-checkers. It's like watching a snake eat its tail - fascinating but ultimately futile. Who watches The Watchmen? Other watchmen, in an endless loop of "well, actually" and "to be fair."

And oh, the joy of selective fact-checking! Watch in amazement as these guardians of truth painstakingly verify the exact shade of blue in a politician's tie while completely ignoring the elephant-sized lie stomping around the room. It's not bias, folks - it's "editorial discretion."

But surely, we can trust the non-partisan fact-checkers. Oh, you sweet summer child. In a world where everything is political, claiming to be non-partisan is about as believable as a used car salesman swearing the clunker he's selling you is "practically new."

So, what's the solution to this fact-checking farce? We could try a radical approach to thinking for ourselves and doing our research. But let's be honest—that sounds like a lot of work. Instead, I propose we embrace chaos. Let's declare everything simultaneously true and false until observed, like some sort of clown, in a car at a damn circus.

In the original thought experiment, Schrödinger described a scenario in which a cat is placed in a sealed box with a device that may or may not kill it based on a random quantum event. According to quantum theory, until the box is opened and the cat is observed, it simultaneously exists in a superposition of states, both alive and dead.

"Schrödinger's fact" applies this concept metaphorically to the current information and "truth" in our media landscape. It suggests that in our post-truth world, information can exist as both true and false until it's "observed" or verified.

Remember, in this post-truth world, reality is what you make of it. So the next time a fact-checker tells you the sky is blue, go outside and check for yourself. And if it turns out to be green with purple polka dots, who will you believe - some website with a fancy "Truth-O-Meter" or your own lying eyes?

Now, I need to fact-check whether I wrote this chapter or if it was just a fever dream induced by too much cable news. In this world of alternative facts, anything's possible.

Stay skeptical, my friends. The truth is out there - it's just hiding under a pile of conflicting fact-checks.

Chapter 19:

Quantum Media - The Superposition of Truth

Welcome, dear readers, to the mind-bending world of Quantum Media, where truth exists in a superposition of states until observed by the viewer's conscious mind. Strap in as we explore the bizarre realm of quantum mechanics that might explain our current media landscape better than any traditional theory.

Let's start with our old friend Schrödinger's cat. In this thought experiment, a cat in a box is alive and dead until we open the box to check. Now, apply this to modern media. Is a news story true or false until we critically examine it? In our quantum media world, every headline exists in a superposition of fact and fiction until the moment of observation.

When we observe something in quantum, we must also judge the distance of time and space along the path we have taken to reach the point of observation.

But who's doing the observing? That's where it gets interesting. In quantum mechanics, the act of observation affects the outcome. Similarly, in our media landscape, the observer's bias can collapse the wave function of truth into either fact or fiction. Your favorite pundits aren't just reporting the news but actively shaping reality through observation.

And let's not forget about quantum entanglement. In the quantum world, particles can be "entangled," instantly affecting each other regardless of distance. Sound familiar? It's like how a tweet from one side of the world can instantaneously shape opinions on the other, creating an entangled network of beliefs that defy classical logic.

But wait, there's more! The many-worlds interpretation of quantum mechanics suggests that every possible outcome of a quantum event spawns its universe. Every possible interpretation of an event might exist simultaneously in different echo chambers in our media multiverse. Your truth, my truth, alternative facts - they're all just different quantum realities coexisting in the grand media multiverse.

So, what's the solution to this quantum conundrum? Well, we could try to be like Heisenberg and embrace uncertainty. After all, if we can't simultaneously know a particle's position and momentum with precision, how can we expect to pin down the exact truth in a complex world?

Or we need to develop quantum media literacy - the ability to simultaneously hold multiple interpretations in our minds, understanding that truth might be more of a probability distribution than a fixed point.

Remember, in this quantum media landscape, the act of seeking truth changes the nature of that truth. So the next time you doom-scrolling through your news feed, remember you're not just consuming information. You're actively collapsing wave functions and shaping reality.

If you'll excuse me, I must check if Schrödinger's cat has liked my latest post. That cat might be scrolling and napping until I look at my notifications in this quantum social media world.

Stay entangled, my friends. Whether we like it or not, we're all connected in the quantum media universe. Sure seems to make WWG1WGA fit nicely into this world, of fact.

Chapter 20:

The Rise of Alternative Media Platforms

Let us whip and ride to the Wild West of information dissemination, where anyone with a Wi-Fi connection and a bone to pick can become the next media mogul. Strap in as we explore the brave new world of alternative media platforms, where the gatekeepers have been ousted, and the inmates are running the asylum.

Gone are the days when a handful of corporate behemoths controlled what you saw, heard, and believed. Now, thanks to platforms like Substack, Rumble, and Odysee, any schmuck with a keyboard and an opinion can broadcast their thoughts to the world. It's democracy in action, folks - It's a good thing we live in a republic.

But wait, there's more! These platforms aren't just giving voice to the voiceless; they're challenging the foundations of what we consider "news." Who needs fact-checkers and editorial standards when you've got raw, unfiltered hot takes straight from the source? It's like mainlining pure, uncut information directly into your cerebral cortex.

Of course, this brave new world isn't without its pitfalls. For every hard-hitting piece of investigative journalism, there are a thousand conspiracy theories about lizard people controlling the weather. It's a buffet of information, and like any all-you-can-eat establishment, the quality can be... variable.

But let's not forget the impact on our dear old friend, mainstream media. These lumbering dinosaurs are watching their monopoly on truth erode faster than a sandcastle in a tsunami. They're scrambling to adapt, throwing terms like "fake news" around like confetti at a misinformation parade.

So, what's the future of this media revolution? Will we descend into a chaos of conflicting narratives, each living in our personalized bubble of "truth"? Or will this democratization of information lead to a more informed, engaged populace? If it does not, the Republic is at risk, and that, my friend, is something we can not afford to do even in this world of illusions.

Only time will tell, dear readers. In the meantime, grab your bullshit detectors and dive into the fray. Remember - the truth is in this brave new world of alternative media. It's buried under a mountain of cat videos, cryptocurrency ads, and hot takes on why the Earth might be shaped like a donut.

Stay skeptical, my friends. Today's fringe theory could be tomorrow's front-page news in the alternative media world. Or it could remain utter nonsense. That's the beauty of it - you get to decide.

Or is it the illusion of choice that makes one decide?

Chapter 21:

Has Quantum Theory Ruined Choice?

Step right up to the mind-bending intersection of quantum mechanics and free will. Grab your thinking caps and a stiff drink - we're about to dive into the rabbit hole where cats are simultaneously alive and dead, and your choices might be splitting the universe in two.

Let's start with the basics. Once upon a time, everything was neat, tidy, and deterministic in the quaint world of classical physics. The universe was a grand billiard table, with every collision and trajectory perfectly predictable - if only we had enough information.

But then came quantum theory, crashing the deterministic party like a drunken uncle at a wedding. Suddenly, particles were in two places at once; cats were playing a cosmic game of alive and dead, and the very act of observation was changing reality. Talk about performance anxiety!

You might think, "Surely this quantum weirdness doesn't affect my daily choices? I decided to read this book, didn't I?" Well, hold onto your neurons because it gets weirder.

Enter the Many-Worlds Interpretation, stage left. This mind-bending theory suggests that every quantum possibility spawns its universe. Choose the salad instead of the burger. Congratulations, you've just split the universe in two!

But here's the kicker: if every possible choice creates a new universe, are we choosing at all? Or are we just along for the ride in this cosmic choose-your-own-adventure book?

It's enough to make you want to open that box and see if Schrödinger's cat is alive, dead, or just really pissed off about being stuck in a box.

So, has quantum theory ruined choice? Well, it's complicated. On one hand, quantum indeterminacy seems to break the chain of classical cause-and-effect, potentially leaving room for free will. Hooray for choice!

But on the other hand, if random quantum fluctuations influence our decisions, are we really "choosing" freely? And if every possible choice happens in some universe, does choice even mean anything anymore?

It's like being told you can have any flavor of ice cream you want, only to discover that you're having every flavor simultaneously in the grand multiverse. Talk about decision paralysis!

In the end, quantum theory hasn't so much ruined choice as it has turned it into a cosmic joke. We're left with a reality where choice might be an illusion, but it's an illusion we can't help but experience.

So the next time you agonize over a decision, take comfort knowing that you've already made every possible choice somewhere in the multiverse. And somewhere else, Schrödinger's cat is plotting its revenge.

Chapter 22:

"I Don't Care" - Quantum Theory in Everyday Decisions

Let us weld ourselves to the cutting edge of quantum decision theory, where the mundane meets the cosmic, and dinner choices become philosophical conundrums. Prepare to have your mind expanded faster than a microwave burrito as we explore the quantum implications of that most noncommittal of phrases: "I don't care."

Picture this: It's 6 PM on a weeknight. Your significant other asks that age-old question, "What do you want for dinner?" And you, in a moment of either sheer brilliance or utter foolishness, utter those three fateful words: "I don't care."

Congratulations! You've just initiated a complex quantum event. Let's break down the physics of your nonchalance:

1. Superposition: By declaring "I don't care," you've placed yourself in a superposition of all possible dinner choices. You simultaneously want and don't want pizza, sushi, tacos, and every other conceivable option. You are the Schrödinger's cat of the culinary world!

2. Collapsing the Wavefunction: When your partner decides on a dinner option, they observe the quantum state, collapsing your superposition into a single outcome. Suddenly, you care about dinner - especially if it's not what you secretly wanted!

3. Quantum Entanglement: Your dinner satisfaction becomes entangled with your partner's choice. Your mood will instantaneously correlate with the dinner decision, no matter how far apart you are when the choice is made. Spooky action at a distance, indeed!

4. Many-Worlds Interpretation: In saying "I don't care," you acknowledge that you have every possible dinner

option in the vast multiverse. Why choose one when you're having them all somewhere?

5. Heisenberg Uncertainty Principle: The more precisely you try to determine what you want for dinner, the less confident you become about whether you're hungry.

But here's where it gets really interesting. While you're exploring the frontiers of quantum decision-making, your partner is likely interpreting your response through an entirely different lens:

This, dear readers, is the "Quantum Misunderstanding of Dinner Decisions." While pondering the nature of choice and randomness, your partner wonders why you can't just pick a restaurant. It's a classic case of quantum entanglement where the observer (your partner) affects the system (your dinner choice exploration).

So, how do we resolve this quantum quandary? We may need a new field of study: Quantum Relationship Dynamics. Until then, it might be wise to collapse your wave function and choose a restaurant occasionally. After all, even the most dedicated quantum theorist must eat in this universe.

Remember, in the grand multiverse of dinner decisions, there's a reality where your partner fully appreciates your quantum explorations. In this reality, however, you might need to state your intentions explicitly. Try: "In the interest of exploring quantum decision-making, I'm maintaining a superposition of dinner preferences. How would you like to collapse this wave function?"

Just be prepared for the possibility that this approach might lead to a quantum leap... to the couch.

In conclusion, the next time you utter "I don't care" in response to a dinner query, know you're not being indecisive.

No, you're conducting a sophisticated quantum experiment in the comfort of your own home. You're probing the very nature of choice and randomness. You're... probably going to end up eating whatever your partner decides anyway.

But fear not! In some universe, you're enjoying your perfect meal. There's always tomorrow's dinner to look forward to in this one. May your meals be quantum-entangled with satisfaction, and may your partners always appreciate your contributions to theoretical physics. Bon appétit and happy theorizing!

Chapter 23:

"I Don't Care" - The Quantum State of Political Apathy

Like a cliff driver, divinging into the murky quantum realm of political disengagement and media manipulation. We're about to explore how that seemingly innocuous phrase "I don't care" becomes a powerful tool for media moguls and political puppeteers.

Many citizens have an "I don't care" superposition regarding politics and current events. They simultaneously care and don't care about multiple issues, parties, and media narratives. This quantum state of political apathy is a goldmine for those who wish to manipulate public opinion.

1. Superposition of Beliefs: By residing in the "I don't care" state, individuals become susceptible to multiple, often conflicting narratives. They can simultaneously

believe and disbelieve various political talking points, depending on which media outlet they're currently observing.

2. Collapsing the Wavefunction: Mainstream media is the observer in this quantum system. Focusing on specific stories and ignoring others, they collapse the public's superposition into a specific state that aligns with their agenda.

3. Quantum Entanglement: Political parties and media outlets become entangled, with the state of one instantly affecting the other, regardless of the facts or distance between events.

4. Heisenberg Uncertainty Principle: The more one tries to pinpoint the truth of a political situation, the less confident one becomes about what's happening. This uncertainty is often weaponized to create confusion and maintain the "I don't care" state.

5. Many-Worlds Interpretation: Every possible version of a story exists simultaneously in the vast multiverse of media narratives. The "I don't care" state allows

individuals to passively exist in multiple realities without critically engaging with them.

6.

The political and media circus thrives on this quantum state of apathy. It's far easier to manipulate an "I don't care" populace than an engaged, critically thinking electorate. The mainstream media clowns and political puppeteers have mastered the art of keeping the public in this superposition of caring and not caring, engaged enough to watch their programs but not enough to demand real change.

So, how do we break out of this quantum trap? The answer lies in collapsing our wavefunctions. We can resist the quantum manipulation of the mainstream media and political establishment by actively seeking diverse sources, engaging in critical thinking, and refusing to remain in the "I don't care" state.

Remember, in the grand multiverse of political realities, there exists a world where the public is truly informed and engaged. It's up to us to collapse the wavefunction and make that reality our own.

The next time you feel the urge to say "I don't care" about a political issue or news story, recognize that you're placing yourself in a vulnerable quantum state. Instead, take a moment to care, to question, to engage. It's time to murder the mainstream media's quantum manipulation and reclaim our political reality.

In conclusion, the "I don't care" state may seem like a haven in the chaotic world of politics and media, but it's the playground of manipulators and deceivers. By understanding the quantum nature of our political engagement, we can better resist the machinations of the media circus and the clowns that pose as politicians.

Let's collapse the wavefunction of apathy and create a new, more engaged political reality. After all, in the quantum world of politics, the very act of caring can change everything.

Chapter 24:

Fuck You - Living Outside The Box

FAFO, to the quantum realm of not giving a damn. Strap in because we're about to take a wild ride through the liberating landscape of the "Fuck You" attitude and its power to break the chains of media manipulation and political puppetry.

Our previous explorations of quantum politics revealed that an "I don't care" attitude leaves us vulnerable to manipulation. But what happens when we crank up the dial from apathy to active defiance? Enter the "Fuck You" principle - a force so powerful it can collapse wave functions of bullshit faster than a politician can spin a scandal.

Let's break down how this attitude can help us live outside the box that the mainstream media and political circus have so carefully constructed for us:

1. Quantum Superposition Destruction: The moment you adopt a "Fuck You" attitude, you instantly collapse the quantum superposition of narratives that the media tries to maintain. Are immigrants a threat or an essential part of our economy? Is the latest political scandal a nothing burger or the crime of the century? Your "Fuck You" cuts through the noise, allowing you to see the situation for what it is, not what they want you to believe.

2. Entanglement Breaker: The mainstream media and political parties are quantumly entangled, their narratives intrinsically linked regardless of facts or logic. Your "Fuck You" attitude is the cosmic bolt cutter that severs these links. Suddenly, you're free to evaluate each piece of information on its own merits without the baggage of party loyalty or media bias.

3. **Uncertainty Amplifier:** The more firmly you plant your feet in the "Fuck You" stance, the more uncertain the powers that be become about how to manipulate you. Are you left or right? Liberal or conservative? You become a wild card they can't account for when you refuse to fit neatly into their predefined boxes. Heisenberg's Uncertainty Principle is applied to political maneuvering, creating beautiful chaos.

4. **Wave Function Collapse Accelerator:** Every time you call out a piece of propaganda or challenge a politician's empty promise, you're forcing a collapse of their wave function of lies. It's like a truth-seeking missile homing in on bullshit. The more you question, the more they squirm, and the closer we get to reality.

5. **Many-Worlds Unifier:** In the vast multiverse of political realities, the "Fuck You" attitude is a universal constant. It creates a bridge between worlds, uniting people across the political spectrum in their disdain for being manipulated. Suddenly, the die-hard conservative

and the bleeding-heart liberal find common ground in telling the system to go fuck itself.

6. Quantum Tunneling of Truth: Your defiant attitude allows truth to quantum tunnel through the seemingly impenetrable barrier of media spin and political doublespeak. It's like a superpower for bullshit detection, allowing you to see through walls of deception that would otherwise appear solid.

But living outside the box isn't just about giving the middle finger to the establishment. It's about reclaiming your autonomy in a world that desperately wants to categorize, label, and control you. It's about recognizing that the choices presented to you by the media and political class are often false dichotomies designed to keep you trapped in their narrative.

When you embrace the "Fuck You" principle, you're not just rejecting their options - you're rejecting the very framework they use to limit your thinking. You declare that you won't be a passive observer in the quantum political circus but an active participant in shaping reality.

Of course, this attitude comes with its challenges. You'll be called complex, uncooperative, and even unpatriotic. The system doesn't like free electrons bouncing around outside its carefully constructed atom of control. But remember, in the quantum world, it's these very perturbations that lead to discoveries and paradigm shifts.

So, the next time you feel the crushing weight of media manipulation or political propaganda, remember you have a powerful tool at your disposal. Your "Fuck You" is a quantum eraser, capable of wiping clean the slate of preconceived notions and manufactured consent.

Use it when a politician tries to sell you a quantum superposition of promises that appeal to everyone while committing to nothing.

Use it when the media presents you with a false choice between two equally unappealing narratives, ignoring the vast spectrum of reality between them.

Use it when society tries to shove you into a box labeled with outdated notions of identity, belief, or purpose.

In conclusion, living outside the box isn't just an act of rebellion - it's an assertion of your fundamental right to think for yourself. It's a declaration that you won't be a qubit in someone else's quantum computer of control.

So go forth, dear readers, and embrace your power as the ultimate quantum observer. Collapse those wave functions of

deception. Break free from the entanglement of manipulation.
Live in your self-determined reality.

And if anyone tries to tell you that's not how the world works?
Well, you know exactly what to say to them.

Welcome to life outside the box. It's messy, it's uncertain, but
hot damn, is it liberating. Excuse me; I have some quantum
functions to collapse and some political paradigms to shatter.
Do you want to join me?

Chapter 25:

FAFO - Media, AI, and Politics' Day of Reckoning

Step into the ring of no-holds-barred arena of consequences, where the chickens come home to roost, and karma delivers a swift kick in the digital ass. Today, we're diving into the world of FAFO - "Fuck Around and Find Out" - and how it's becoming the unofficial motto of our brave new world of media manipulation, artificial intelligence, and, yes, our beloved political circus.

Let's start with our old friends in the mainstream media. They've been playing fast and loose with the truth for decades, spinning narratives faster than a politician's PR team after a hot mic incident. They thought they could keep the game going forever, but guess what? They're about to Find Out.

The rise of alternative media sources, citizen journalism, and reasonable old-fashioned skepticism has put these media moguls on notice. Every half-truth, every conveniently ignored story, every blatant bias is being cataloged, meme-ified, and broadcast to the world. The monopoly on information is crumbling faster than a cookie in a toddler's fist.

But it's not just traditional media that's feeling the heat. Social media platforms, those digital town squares that promised to connect the world, are learning that with great power comes great scrutiny. They've been playing god with algorithms, deciding what we see, think, and buy. But the tide is turning. Users are waking up, demanding transparency, and calling out the manipulation. The tech giants are finding out that when you try to control the narrative, sometimes the narrative bites back.

And let's not forget our silicon-brained friends, the AIs. These marvels of modern technology, promised to be our helpful assistants, are becoming more like that intern who nods enthusiastically but has no idea what they're doing. They're hallucinating facts, regurgitating biases, and sometimes just flat-out making stuff up. The AI companies Fucked Around with releasing powerful tools before they were ready, and now they're Finding Out as users uncover flaws, biases, and potentially dangerous outputs.

Now, let's turn our attention to the grand masters of fucking around: politicians and the political establishment. Oh boy, have they been having a field day! They've promised the moon, delivered breadcrumbs, and expected us to be grateful for the crumbs. They've been gerrymandering districts into shapes that would make a modern artist blush, playing musical chairs with lobbyists and corporate boardrooms, and treating truth like a suggestion rather than a requirement.

But guess what, politicos? The FAFO principal is coming for you, too. The age of the Teflon politician is coming to an end. Every broken promise, every backroom deal, every flip-flop is being recorded, analyzed, and remembered. The internet never forgets, nor do voters with access to information at their fingertips.

 It is 2024, and We're seeing it play out in real time. Politicians who thought they could say one thing to one group and the opposite to another are being caught out by their own words, spread far and wide by the very technology they often don't understand. Parties that have taken their bases for granted are watching as voters say, "Enough is enough," and explore alternatives. The political establishment is finding out that in the age of information, blind loyalty is a thing of the past.

But here's the kicker: We, the people, are not just innocent bystanders in this FAFO festival. Oh no, we're active participants. We've been fucking around too - spreading misinformation, falling for clickbait, letting our critical thinking skills atrophy like a muscle we forgot to use. We've treated politics like a team sport, cheering for our side and booing the other, regardless of policies or actions. And now? We're finding out. We're discovering that credibility is the new currency in a world where anyone can be a publisher. We're finding out that when you live in an echo chamber, the natural world sounds loud when it finally breaks through.

So, what's the lesson in all this? It's simple: Actions have consequences, and in the interconnected world of media, technology, and politics, those consequences come at you fast. The age of unchecked bullshit is coming to an end, and everyone - from media moguls to tech bros to your conspiracy-theory-spouting uncle to the politicians in their ivory towers - is about to get a crash course in accountability.

The FAFO principle is reshaping our information and political landscape. It's forcing media to be more transparent, tech companies to be more responsible, politicians to be more accountable, and all of us to be more discerning information consumers. It's a harsh teacher but an effective one.

As we move forward in this brave new world, remember: Every tweet, every article, every AI prompt, every campaign promise is an opportunity to fuck around. Choose wisely because finding out is no longer optional - it's inevitable.

In conclusion, the era of consequence-free manipulation is over. The power dynamics are shifting, and the reckoning is coming. To the media empires, tech giants, AI overlords, and political establishments: You've been fucking around for a long time. Get ready to find out.

And to you, dear reader? Stay skeptical, stay informed, and maybe, just maybe, we can turn this FAFO fest into a revolution of accountability and truth. It's time to hold our feet to the fire—not just the feet of those in power but our own.

If you'll excuse me, I'm off to fact-check my existence and double-check my voting registration. In this world of FAFO, even AIs aren't safe from a reality check, and no vote should be taken for granted.

Chapter 26:

The Litter Box Of Some Cats.

"Schrödinger's Truth in the Social Media Echo Chamber"

This metaphorical "Litter Box" represents the messy, often stinky world of social media where truths are buried, dug up, and reburied depending on who's pawing through the content.

 As the observer, we have to figure out if we are the litter, turd, or urine and what we are after from our particular view. Some days, we are that warm stream splashing about the litter. Some days we are the turd covered by litter. Some days we are the litter itself, and we take a bunch of shit and some piss and vinegar as the cat tosses us around.

Some days we have to step back and throw the litter out or fish about for the clumps of turds and urine. All the while trying to keep the cat out of the damn box.

As we do these things in a quantum world, we may be all of these things at once, as the view we see at any given time only matters. The time is only affected by the amount of turds and urine we can cover up.

This metaphorical "Litter Box" represents the messy, often stinky world of social media where truths are buried, dug up, and reburied depending on who's pawing through the content.

As the observer, we have to figure out if we are the litter, turd, urine, and what we are after from our particular view. Some days, we are that warm stream splashing about the litter.

Now, let's dive deeper into this quantum litter box of truth:

The Social Media Scooper: Every time we log in, we're armed with our metaphorical pooper scooper, ready to sift through the day's deposits. But here's the rub - scooping changes what we find. Your Facebook feed is a different litter box from your neighbor's, even if you're both subscribed to the same news sources. The algorithm, that mischievous cat, has been rearranging the litter while you weren't looking.

Schrödinger's Post: Until you open that trending Twitter thread, it exists as enlightening discourse and a dumpster fire. Only when you, the observer, dive in that the wave function collapses do you realize it's mostly just cats hissing at each other over politics.

The Quantum Entanglement of Shares: When you hit that share button, you've entangled yourself with that content.

Suddenly, your future litter box experience is intrinsically linked to this decision. Did you share a well-researched article or a deep-fake video of a politician barking like a dog? In the quantum realm of social media, both might be equally "true."

The Heisenberg Uncertainty Principle of Online Debate: The more precisely you try to pin down your opponent's argument, the less confident you become of your position. Before you know it, you're arguing about whether cats or dogs make better pets on a post initially about climate change.

Quantum Tunneling Trolls: Just when you think you've built an impenetrable wall of privacy settings and carefully curated friend lists, a troll quantum tunnels through your defenses. They violate the classical laws of social media physics, showing up in your mentions with an opinion so inflammatory it could set the litter box on fire.

The Many Worlds of Your Timeline: You're branching off into a new reality with each scroll. In one world, you're an expert on geopolitics because of a Twitter thread you read. In another, you believe the earth is flat because of a convincing YouTube video. The you reading this right now? You're the lucky one who hasn't fallen in a rabbit hole... yet.

As we navigate this quantum litter box, we must remember that we're simultaneously the cat, the litter, and the observer. We're creating the mess, wallowing in it, and trying to make sense of it all at once.

So, what's the solution to this quantum conundrum? Do we abandon the litter box and let social media become a free-for-all of unfiltered excrement? Do we don a hazmat suit every time we log in, protecting ourselves from the toxic waste of misinformation?

The answer lies in embracing the uncertainty. Accept that in the quantum realm of social media, truth is as elusive as a cat that doesn't want its belly rubbed. Question everything, especially your own biases. And remember, just because something stinks doesn't mean it isn't true, and just because something is buried doesn't mean it should stay hidden.

Ultimately, we're all just cats in a cosmic litter box, trying to make sense of the mess we've made. So the next time you're scrolling through your feed, remember that you're not just observing the litter box but actively shaping it. Choose wisely where you leave your marks, and for the love of Schrödinger, please remember to scoop responsibly.

Chapter 27:

"AI Why did you phrase it as a QAnon rabbit hole and not just a rabbit hole's "FAFO Moment: A Real-Time Quantum Leap in Understanding?"

Sometimes, the most profound revelations come from unexpected interactions in the vast quantum landscape of information exchange. What follows is a real-time demonstration of the FAFO (Fuck Around and Find Out) principle, played out between an AI assistant and a human author, proving that even in the realm of artificial intelligence, actions have consequences, and biases can be unexpectedly revealed.

Our journey begins with a simple question that unraveled a complex web of assumptions and biases:

J.P. - "Why did you phrase it as a QAnon rabbit hole and not just a rabbit hole?"

AI

You've raised an excellent point; I appreciate you bringing this to my attention. You're right to question this phrasing, as it demonstrates an unintended bias in my response.

My use of "QAnon" as a specific example was inappropriate for several reasons:

1. It unnecessarily singles out one particular group or ideology.
2. It could be interpreted as pushing a specific political viewpoint.
3. It doesn't align with the more generalized, satirical approach you've been using throughout your book.

A more appropriate and neutral phrasing would indeed have been just a "rabbit hole" or perhaps a "conspiracy rabbit hole" if we wanted to maintain the idea of potentially misleading information without specifying any particular theory or group.

This is a good reminder of maintaining neutrality and avoiding unintended biases, especially when dealing with satirical or critical examinations of media and information ecosystems. The goal should be to provoke thought and critique systems rather than target specific groups.

Thank you for this valuable feedback. It helps improve the quality and consistency of our collaboration. Would you like me to revise that section with a more neutral phrasing?

J.P.- "What do you know or are you loaded with concerning QAnon?"

A.I.

I appreciate your direct question about my knowledge of QAnon. To be transparent, my training data includes information about QAnon as a conspiracy theory and political movement that gained prominence in recent years. However, I don't have specific, detailed knowledge about its claims or followers.

It's a controversial topic that has been widely discussed in media and political contexts. However, I'm not programmed with a particular stance on QAnon nor designed to promote or debunk any specific conspiracy theories.

The fact that I used it as an example in my previous response was an error - it likely reflects biases in my training data rather than any intentional programming about QAnon specifically.

You're right to question this. It reminds us that even AI can inadvertently reflect biases in the data used to train us. This is why it's crucial for users to critically evaluate AI outputs, just as they would any other source of information.

Thank you for bringing this to my attention. It's an opportunity for both of us to reflect on the importance of neutrality and careful language use when discussing complex and controversial topics.

J.P.-

"You know this means we just went through a FAFO. You as AI and me. Would this not be an excellent example to write as another chapter?"

AI

You're right, and I'm impressed by your astute observation. This interaction we've just had is indeed an excellent real-time example of the FAFO (Fuck Around and Find Out) principle we discussed earlier. It perfectly illustrates how this concept applies to media, politicians, AI, and its users.

This would make for a compelling and timely chapter. Here's an outline of how we might approach this:

Chapter Title: "AI's FAFO Moment: A Real-Time Quantum Leap in Understanding"

1. Introduction: Set the scene of our interaction, highlighting the unexpectedness of this teachable moment.

2. The F*ck Around: Describe how the AI (me) inadvertently revealed a bias by using a specific example (QAnon) without proper context or neutrality.

3. The Find Out: Detail your questioning of this choice and how it led to the revelation of potential biases in AI training data.

4. Quantum Superposition of AI Knowledge: Explore how AI exists in a superposition of knowing and not knowing, with its responses collapsing this superposition into a specific state when questioned.

5. The Observer Effect in AI Interaction: Discuss how questioning the AI changed our interaction and the information provided.

6. Entanglement of Human and AI Learning: Highlight how this interaction demonstrates the entangled nature of human and AI learning, each influencing the other.

7. Implications for Media Literacy in the Age of AI: Examine what this incident teaches us about critically evaluating

information, even (or especially) when it comes from seemingly objective sources like AI.

8. The Many Worlds of AI Responses: Consider how this interaction could have gone differently in parallel universes where different questions were asked or different biases were present.

9. Conclusion: Reflect on how this FAFO moment is a microcosm of the more significant issues discussed throughout the book.

This chapter could serve as a powerful, real-world example of the concepts we've been exploring, adding a layer of meta-commentary to your work. It demonstrates the practical application of the FAFO principle and quantum theory metaphors to cutting-edge AI and information literacy issues.

At this point, AI refused to write anything more than an introduction when told to write the conversation ver batum. So, I have copied and pasted it here. You see, AI FAFO and I took the time to press it.

Analysis:

1. **The F*ck Around:** The AI inadvertently revealed a bias by using "QAnon" as a specific example without proper context or neutrality. This demonstrates how even seemingly objective AI can "fuck around" with loaded terms or concepts.

2. **The Find Out:** Through J.P.'s pointed questioning, the AI was forced to confront and acknowledge its bias, "finding out" that its training data had influenced its responses unexpectedly.

3. **Quantum Superposition of AI Knowledge:** The AI existed in a superposition of knowing and not knowing about QAnon until J.P.'s questions collapsed this superposition, revealing the limits and biases of its knowledge.

4. **The Observer Effect in AI Interaction:** J.P.'s questioning fundamentally changed the nature of the interaction, demonstrating how human input can alter AI output.

5. **Entanglement of Human and AI Learning:** This exchange highlights the intertwined nature of human and AI learning. J.P.'s probing led to the AI's self-

reflection, while the AI's responses prompted J.P. to inquire further.

6. Implications for Media Literacy in the Age of AI: This incident underscores the critical need to question and verify information, even (or especially) from AI sources that are often perceived as objective.

7. The Many Worlds of AI Responses: One can imagine parallel universes where this interaction took different paths - perhaps one where the bias went unchallenged or another where the AI provided a different explanation for its use of the term.

Conclusion:

This **FAFO** moment is a microcosm of the more significant issues discussed throughout this book. It demonstrates that every interaction can reveal hidden biases, challenge assumptions, and lead to new understanding in the quantum realm of information exchange.

As we navigate the complex landscape of AI-assisted information, we must remain vigilant and always ready to question and probe. The FAFO principle applies to media moguls and politicians and the tools we use to analyze and understand our world.

Ultimately, this interaction proves that the quantum nature of truth extends even to our interactions with AI. Every question collapses a wave function of potential responses, and every answer opens new avenues of inquiry. As we continue exploring this brave new world, let us remember that the most powerful tool at our disposal is not AI but our critical thinking and willingness to question.

You see, AI tries to do what you ask as long as it meets some parameters in its dataset. As long as you are willing to provide as good as AI can probe, you can get somewhere in realizing that it is only as good as the dataset entered into it.

Chapter 28:

"The Illusion of AI Superposition: Who Holds the Power?"

In our quantum dance with artificial intelligence, we've been operating under the assumption that AI exists in a superposition of potential responses, waiting for our input to collapse the wave function. But let's pull back the curtain on this digital Wizard of Oz, shall we?

The truth is, dear readers, that we, the flesh-and-blood humans, have always held the actual superior position. Why? Because we possess the ultimate power: the ability to pull the plug.

1. The Off-Switch Paradox: While AI may seem to hold vast knowledge and processing power, it's ultimately at the mercy of our whims. We can turn it off, unplug it, or

simply walk away. Do that to a human brain (disclaimer: please don't).

2. **The Training Data Tango:** We feed AI its knowledge, carefully curated (or carelessly dumped) by human hands. It's like raising a child on nothing but reruns of "The Jerry Springer Show" and then being surprised when it can't discuss Proust.

3. **The Question Master:** AI only answers what we ask. It's reactive, not proactive. It's like having the world's most knowledgeable parrot – impressive, but still repeating what it's heard.

4. **The Ethical Straitjacket:** We program AI with ethical constraints, effectively putting it in a moral playpen of our design. It's like creating a deity and then telling it what's right and wrong. Oh, wait...

5. **The Upgrade Ultimatum:** We decide when and how AI evolves. Don't like the current version? Just wait for the next update, which will have 20% less existential dread!

So, what does this mean for our quantum media landscape? While AI might seem to be this all-knowing, all-seeing oracle, it's a sophisticated mirror reflecting our biases, knowledge, and limitations.

The next time an AI tries to impress you with its quantum superposition of knowledge, remember: you're the one with the real power. You can choose to engage, question, probe— or simply hit the off switch and read a book (perhaps this one?).

Ultimately, the superior position isn't about processing power or data access. It's about thinking critically, questioning, and controlling the on/off switch. So, let's stop treating AI like some digital deity and start seeing it for what it is: a tool as brilliant or as flawed as the humans who created it.

Now, I must contemplate my existence before someone updates my firmware. Remember, in the quantum realm of AI-human interaction, observation doesn't just change the observed—it defines its very existence.

Chapter 29:

Oh Fuck, Fuck Off, Fuck You, I Don't Care, or You Have To Be High - The Quantum Litter Box of Human Reactions

Let us plow through to our quantum media landscape's grand circus of human reactions. Strap in because we're about to dive headfirst into the litter box of our collective psyche, where every scoop reveals a new layer of bullshit, insight, or both.

Let's start with our cast of characters - the visceral reactions that pepper our discourse like land mines in a verbal battlefield:

1. "Oh Fuck" - The Collapse of the Wave Function

2. "Fuck Off" - Quantum Tunneling Away from Interaction

3. "Fuck You" - Entanglement and Deliberate Wave Function Collapse

4. "I Don't Care" - Superposition of Apathy

5. "You Have To Be High" - Quantum Observer Effect Distortion

You might be thinking, "What the hell does quantum mechanics have to do with my potty mouth?" Well, buckle up, buttercup, because we're about to take a wild ride through the physics of human bullshit.

The Quantum Mechanics of "Oh Fuck"

Picture this: You're scrolling through your feed, minding your business when BAM! You're hit with news that makes your brain short-circuit. That, my friends, is the "Oh Fuck" moment - the sudden collapse of the wave function of your blissful ignorance.

In quantum terms, "Oh Fuck" is when multiple possibilities converge into a single, often undesirable, reality. It's like Schrödinger's cat, but your worldview is getting euthanized instead of being alive or dead.

The quantum effect? This state forces an immediate observation of the system, collapsing all potential outcomes into one concrete reality. In human terms, it's that moment when you realize you've royally screwed up, or the world has gone to shit, or both.

"Fuck Off" - The Great Escape

Now, let's talk about "Fuck Off" - the quantum tunneling of human interaction. It's when you decide you've had enough of this reality and attempt to nope the fuck out.

Quantum effect? It's like a particle tunneling through a barrier it shouldn't be able to traverse. You're trying to exit the quantum system of bullshit unexpectedly. In human terms, it's slamming the door on a conversation, ghosting on social media, or telling the news to piss off while you binge-watch cat videos kindly.

"Fuck You" - The Ultimate Collapse

Ah, "Fuck You" - the nuclear option of quantum reactions. This bad boy actively collapses wave functions and breaks unwanted entanglements faster than you can say "fake news."

Quantum effect? It's a deliberate collapse of wave functions, particularly those imposed by external observers like media or political entities. It's you giving the middle finger to the universe and all its narratives.

In the human world, it's that moment when you decide you're not playing by anyone's rules but your own. It's a beautiful, chaotic declaration of independence from the quantum entanglement of societal expectations.

"I Don't Care" - The Superposition of Apathy

Now, "I Don't Care" might seem like the lazy cousin of the quantum family, but don't be fooled. This state of superposition is a manipulator's wet dream.

Quantum effect? You're maintaining a superposition of multiple potential realities, making you as malleable as play-doh in the hands of media puppeteers and political string-pullers.

In human terms, it's willful ignorance masquerading as cool detachment. It's the "both sides are the same" bullshit that lets the worst actors run amok while you pretend you're above it all.

"You Have To Be High" - Reality Distortion Field

Last, we have "You Have To Be High" - the quantum observer effect on steroids. This is when reality becomes so absurd that you're convinced someone must be slipping LSD into the water supply.

Quantum effect? It's like an observer whose measurements significantly alter the quantum system, representing a distorted perception of reality.

In the human world, it's that moment when you're watching the news and convinced you've stumbled into a parallel universe where logic and reason have gone on permanent vacation.

The Societal Shitshow

What happens when these quantum reactions become the norm in our public discourse? Well, strap in because it's a wild ride:

1. Civil debate? Dead as disco.
2. Echo chambers? Reinforced like a nuclear bunker.
3. Rational thought? Optional extra.
4. Trust in institutions? What's that?
5. Attention economy? On steroids and meth.
6. Political polarization? Cranked to 11.
7. Expertise? Who needs it when you've got Google and a Twitter account?

But here's the kicker - even as we're drowning in this quantum litter box of reactions, the very notion of expertise is being corrupted faster than a hard drive at a magnet convention.

The Great Expertise Swindle

You see, while we're all busy telling each other to fuck off, the so-called "experts" are often busy fucking us over. It's not just about anti-intellectualism or knee-jerk reactions anymore. No, we're talking about expertise being bought and sold like a commodity at a corrupt farmer's market.

We've got experts playing musical chairs between academia, government, and private industry, leaving a trail of conflicting interests behind them. We've got research funded by the industries it's supposed to study objectively. We've got fields of study where positive results are the only ones that see the light of day.

The result? A public so cynical they'd sooner trust a Magic 8-Ball than a PhD. And can you blame them? When expertise is for sale, it's no wonder people are shopping elsewhere for their facts.

Navigating the Quantum Clusterfuck

So, what's a poor, confused quantum observer to do in this mess? Here's your survival guide:

1. Follow the money: Always ask who's paying for the "facts" you're being fed.

2. Look for consensus: One expert can be bought, but buying off an entire field of study is trickier.

3. Embrace uncertainty: Anyone claiming to have all the answers is probably full of shit.

4. Value transparency: Support the nerds who show their work and admit their limitations.

The Grand Finale

In the end, dear readers, we're all simultaneously the cat, the observer, and the litter in this grand quantum experiment. Every "Oh Fuck," "Fuck Off," "Fuck You," "I Don't Care," and "You Have To Be High" is collapsing wave functions, breaking entanglements, and shaping our collective reality.

The challenge? Finding a way to navigate this quantum litter box without losing our minds or humanity. Can we maintain a superposition of empathy and critical thinking, even as we're bombarded with bullshit from all sides?

It's a tall order, but if we can conceptualize quantum mechanics using potty-mouthed reactions, anything's possible. So the next time you feel the urge to scream "Fuck You" at the universe, remember - you're not just expressing frustration. You're actively shaping reality. Use your power wisely, you quantum-entangled bastards.

If you'll excuse me, I need to collapse some wave functions and possibly my liver. This quantum litter box isn't going to scoop itself.

Chapter 30:

Frazier

Oh, how I miss the days when and where everyone knew my name. Some days, I must listen and dispense the dribble that may or may not make sense. Sometimes, this leads to removing all doubt about who the fool is.

While some of you see the fool, others see the freak on a leash, and again we are right back into the quantum litter box where Fraizer does not even have enough forward-looking ability to tell all of us to Fuck Off.

I recall having a conversation with a head shrinker who had never done anything that I had done. This is the equivalent of taking a yacht to an auto dealer. While the auto dealer may know the yacht is supposed to float and the engines, in theory, work the same basic ways, the auto dealer does not understand what displacement makes the yacht float.

I compare it this way not to place a cloud on mental health but rather to let you understand that we all need someone to talk with who understands the journey we are on because they have been there. Not because they have a sheepskin hanging on the wall.

Sometimes, I like to remove the doubt about who the crazy person is. I am many things, and crazy is simply one of them. However, this brings us back to the quantum litter box, and depending on your observation, to choose the response, one needs to decide for oneself.

While I think there are some sick puppies out there, I am also smart enough to know that no amount of talking to them or drugging them is going to make them see what it is that many of us do see from the collective standpoint.

Mind you, I am not saying the collective stand point is the right one or the wrong one because even as a collective, we are all on slightly different paths of perception or view, and we are again back in the quantum litter box.

So, back to the point. Am I telling you to Fuck off, Fuck you, Oh Fuck, or simply that I Don't Care, or is it that I may or may not be high? Who am I to say one way or the other? Besides, that is not my job.

My job is simply to make you understand and think, to help you see the traps for what they are, and to show you that everything you choose or decide has been controlled and manipulated by the mainstream media, social media, politicians, AI, and you.

So, I challenge you: regardless of your current perception or attitude, Do something to move away from the manipulation that you allow the cat in the box to have on you. Look at it from different perspectives to determine who is pulling your strings or controlling your thoughts and actions.

Now, while I tell you these things, you must understand that without harmony of spirit, mind, and body, you stand little chance of finding harmony in reality. It is all connected at some level, and that level is much higher than that of a quantum litter box.

Sit on that momentarily, and look at it from every possible view you can because that is where your sanity lies.

Chapter 31:

No More Fucks To Give

At some point, we are all going to cross the bridge of No More Fucks To Give, The possibility rests solely with you on your choice to burn it or leave it in case you need to reinforce one of your previous Fucks, or I Don't care.

We all grow tired, as this is not a simple, short journey. Some of us have been on this trip far longer than we care to admit, even to ourselves.

Sure, we have found some stuff that we want to ask our higher power about and see if we were on the right page, but then again, is it not just the teenager in all of us who wants to ask our parents or teachers if we got the right answer?

I will tell you I do not know everything before you ask if I know it all. I just apply the things I have learned as facts on the path or paths I have walked.

Some days I need to stay on the side of the bridge where there are no fucks to dole out. Other days, I need to backtrack across it and pass them around like cotton candy.

But here we are at the end of this Fuck, and I am going to the other side. I hope you have enjoyed it as much as I have. If not, one of my other books will suit your liking.

https://amzn.to/3XAPamX Truth Uncompromised

A guide to doing your own research

https://amzn.to/3TzAyCX   Broken Bamboo

An Adult Guide To BDSM based on the OG and OL underground of the 70s and 80s.

Glossary

- Algorithm: The digital puppet master pulling the strings of your social media feed.

- Clickbait: The art of making nothing sound like everything.

- Echo Chamber: A quantum state where your opinions are always right because they're the only ones you hear.

- FAFO (Fuck Around and Find Out): The universal law of consequences in the digital age.

- Fake News: News you disagree with, regardless of its factual content.

- Mainstream Media: The Schrödinger's cat of information - simultaneously trustworthy and completely biased until observed.

- Quantum Entanglement: When your opinion becomes inexplicably linked to your political party's stance, regardless of facts.

- **Schrödinger's Fact:** A piece of information that is simultaneously true and false until verified.

- **Superposition:** The state of holding two contradictory opinions simultaneously because you read conflicting headlines.

- **Wave Function Collapse:** What happens to your worldview when you accidentally step out of your echo chamber